From the Mind of an Inr
"Escaping Men

MW00882036

Written by: Herbert L. Fields

Copyright © 2015 by Herbert L. Fields

All rights reserved. Printed in the United States of America

Publishing services by JMC Publishing www.janeidechillis.com
Createspace/Amazon Email: janeidechillis@gmail.com

Chief Editor: Vivian S. Matthews

Graphics Designer: Ashley Photographik Cleveland

www.kreativekaptures.com

www.jmcpublishing1.com

ISBN – 13: 978-1518710179

ISBN – 10:1518710174

No part of this publication may be reproduced, stored in a retrieval system or transmitted in any way by any means, electronic, mechanical, photocopying, recording or otherwise, without the permission of the author except as provided by the USA copyright law.

From the Mind of an Inner City Black Man:
Escaping Mental Slavery

Chapters:

Dedication:

This book is dedicated to my children Ashley Jason and Zoe who inspire me everyday. To my brother Michael Fields who was the writer in the family. Mike, the poet as we called him passed away in 2002. He never got the chance to express the deep things he had inside of him. Also, to my mother Elizabeth Fields, my friend who raised me, taught me and kept me out of danger. She is a strong woman, and I'm blessed to have her as my mom. Lastly, to God my Father who gives me strength to do all things, and all the men and women who died trying to express themselves and didn't know how.

Introduction:

The purpose of the book is to give you a road map for change. It does not matter what color you are, or if you live in the inner city or in the country. The principles in this book will help you to see clearly the things around you that can't be seen. But they stop you from growing and getting ahead in life. The principles in this book are provided to point you in the right direction and give you the tools to be productive in todays up side down world. It will also help to reclaim your minds by reestablishing your self-esteem. It will help you to form habits. Habits are formed when three things are in place. 1. Having knowledge to do a thing. 2. Knowing why to do a thing. 3. And knowing the benefits of doing a thing. When all three are in place a habit is easy to be formed. These good habits will uplift, motivate and inspire you to work on relationship skills and interpersonal skills that most people have a hard time with. This book will help with focusing, which in turn will bring about a change in the lives of men and woman in their community, in their city, their families. Most men if you could ask them, who are you could not tell you because they don't know. So I ask you this question, who are you?

- *Miles Monroe* said, "It is not bad to have time, it is bad to not know why and what to do with the time. A man or woman who do not know who they are will wonder aimlessly through life trying to find their way."

Chapter 1# - Who are you?

I use to struggle with that question every day; saying to myself it has got to be more to life than what I am doing. My life was going nowhere fast. I was on drugs. I was doing badly in school. I had a problem with my anger. I was a sex addict. Pornographic movies and pornographic books was my favorite past time. My life was all messed up. The reality was I didn't know anything was wrong. I thought it was normal and everyone did this kind of stuff. I believed I didn't have a problem with drugs; the people who think I have a problem had the problem. My thinking was wrong. I use to call myself the devils son-in-law. I believed that I was. I use to like to hurt people. I remember one time in my life I use to like the taste of tears when I made someone cry.

A girlfriend I would taste her tears and it was good. I liked it! Sick don't you think! The gang I used to be in thought nothing of walking down the street and seeing a stranger and beating him up and laughing about it later. I hated anyone to tell me what to do, even my mom. My father was never around. He left when I was five. That is another story we will get to that another time. My mom told me if I can't live by her rules, I had to go. So I did. I left home and got my own place with my younger 15-year-old brother. It was a bad mistake.

It was drugs, sex and alcohol everyday. I was still at Eastside High School; I would go to school when, and if I felt like it. My life was out of control. I had no direction. Whatever felt good, I would do it. I am thankful to God I am not dead. Some days I would wake up and not know were I was and how I got there. The sad thing was I had a lot of company. All my friends around me were doing this. I was lost I believed wrong was right and right was wrong. I didn't know who I was. Take a moment look at your life and your habits and what is in control of your life then ask youself where are you going and who are you?

Chapter #2 Questions in my mind:

1. Who am I?
2. Why don't I understand?
3. Why does it hurt so much?
4. How can I make it out of the ghetto?
5. Why me?
6. Why are they so afraid of Black men?
7. Why am I so poor?
8. Why are others so rich?
9. Why do my friends die so young?
10. Why are the rest of them in jail?
11. Why don't they see what I see?
12. Why don't they care?
13. Why can't someone do something about it?
14. Why is my school so dirty?
15. Why don't my teachers care?
16. Why am I treated so badly?
17. Why are my streets so dirty around my house?
18. Why there are 10 liquor stores on one street?
19. Why are there so many drugs?
20. Why do the cops ride past the drug dealers and not stop?
21. Why are there so many churches?
22. Why are they not helping?
23. Why doesn't God come around on my block?
24. Where is His power on earth?
25. Why don't we have a play ground without broken glass all over it?
26. Why don't we have enough to eat?
27. Why can't I sleep at night with all the noise?
28. Why can't I get my thoughts together?
29. Why am I here?
30. What am I to do with my life?
31. Why do I feel like screaming?
32. Why do so many people drops out of school?
33. Why are there no jobs for me?
34. Why is my father not around?
35. Why are people ignoring me?
36. Why can't they see I need help?
37. Why are babies having babies?

38. Why is my mom on welfare?
39. Why is it easier to get help from the government if my wife leaves me?
40. Why can't they help us stay together?
41. Why are all the libraries in my town closing?
42. Why all these questions, and yet I have no answers?
43. WHY?

With all these questions and no answers how can I feel like a man? With all the strikes against me how can I feel that I can make it? Sometimes I felt like giving up, ending it all. It would be like a tree falling in the forest-no one would know I fell. I am an invisible man – a threat to society. I was a danger to myself my family, and friends. I am a product that some use to make money off of. They put me in a position were I can't win and put me in jail for trying to help myself. I can't get a good job because I couldn't read. I graduated from high school but I can't balance a checkbook. My mind was being control by what I saw and what I saw had me out of control. How would you expect me to be?

Chapter #3 Who am I?

What a question. I look deep inside my mind trying to fine out. I hear people call me a lot of things. Am I a nigger, am I lost, am I hopeless, and am I a slave. Some call me, stupid, some women call me a dog and it was bad. Today my friends call me dog and it's okay. When I was growing up they called me Black, and African American. When some one called me a nigger it was time to fight. Today they call me nigger and it's all right. I must go back to my roots. Let me see my grandfather was a slave, a breeder not horses or cows, he bread little black workers in the field. I guess that is where the dog came from. Did you know you could be taught to act a certain way and pass it on to your children? My father has 20 + children all by different women. I did not meet my father until I was in my mid 30's. Growing up I had the same traits like my father. After 30 years I found out that I was someone I thought I was not.

The man I thought was my father was not. It made me think who am I? This is a question many people are afraid to ask. When we do ask questions we become overwhelmed by some of the answers. By breeding we have been taught not to deal with problems (Black men) but to ignore them and it will go away. That is why there are so many "babies' daddies" around. We are so called man enough to make them, however, we run from the responsibility that comes with them. It is too much work. I thank God that my only children are by the woman I married – and that was God. We were taught the more women you get with the more of a man you were. What a Lie! I realize that being with so many different women messed me up! Sex is not just a physical act it's spiritual as well. Giving yourself to someone sexually make you and that person one. You take in their spirit and everyone else they may have been with. They take your spirit, and everyone else that you been with. In other words your spirit becomes contaminated.

You have too many different people inside of you blocking things out. Important things like people feelings and you hurting other people for pleasure your own. It becomes a way of life in all areas and before you know it you can't help yourself. You become a slave to your passions and others passions that's why we become so good at living a lie. We lose sight of the truth. Look at our children today calling each other nigger.

If you ask them what it means, they won't know the true meaning, ignorant! Some people know this and still do it.

We have learned to think right is wrong and wrong is right. We have learned this lesson well. Just look at our young men and communities and you will see how good we are at blocking out the problems. In the city of Paterson the biggest business is young inner city men and women. They are victims of the system. It's just getting bigger and bigger. The jails and detention homes are all full. Someone is getting rich and our kids are the products being sold as slave to the unfair exchange system. When I walk down 12th Avenue and 10th Avenue and see all the young men on the corner, it makes me angry because it is not happening in other cities like Fairlawn and Ridgewood. Why? Because the powers to be in those towns will not let it happen. It's stopped at the first sign of trouble. Why not in Paterson? We have more cops and more money in taxes?

I place a lot of the blame on the churches. They have the power and will not use it. Its not about us, it's about them and their programs within the church. What about what's taking place outside, and all around them? If they would come together and be the church they called themselves to be, this city and others would be a better place to live. It makes me want to cry. Then I ask myself what can I do to help? Little me who am I? How could one person make a difference in the lives of so many? I realized if I am not a part of the solution, I am the problem. It is like going into the barbershop or salon and hearing the problems in the community.

Everyone knows the problems but no one is willing to do anything to change it because they think; what could one person do? A single candle in a dark room makes a big difference. At least you can see where you are going. The Empire State Building was built one brick at a time. Do what you can and you will see a difference.

Let's get back to my question. Who am I? I grew up in the Christopher Columbus Projects (CCP). Life in the projects was extremely hard. It was like being in jail with a little more freedom. As a child, I have seen some things that children should not see. Like my best friend being shot in the head and dead drug addict with needles still in their arms in the stairway of my building, small children eating out of garbage cans and of course rat infested apartments throughout the buildings. In one of my friends houses, the rats made tunnels through all their furniture and made their homes in the beds of the children. There were also so many roaches. It looked as if the walls in our home were alive and constantly moving. Many times children had no food. Many time children were found dead, beaten and raped. Some nights it was so sad, all I could do was cry because I wanted to get out of there. However, it was the only world I knew. I remember wondering if any black people lived in houses like the Brady Bunch on TV and had little or no problems like them such as "what should I wear to school today." Why do I have to play on streets with broken glass all over it? Sometime I would sit by my window at night and just listen to the fights. I wonder who's going to die tonight. Growing up in this type of surrounding either makes you stronger or weaker. I guess its how I learned to block out the bad things I saw all around me. Like passing someone on the ground bleeding and not caring or stopping to help. That behavior is not natural; however it is a learned behavior for a lot of people in the hood.

This is how we are conditioned to be and it has a way of numbing us to our surrounding. To see drug dealers on the block, selling to kids and parents just walking by and not calling the police. This is just the way things were and we couldn't do anything about it. That's a lie. As people who pay to live in a place we have a right to do something about it. If we don't and our children and grandchildren get on drugs then we must blame ourselves. Thinking that it will go away or that's just the way it is, is wrong. We must stop fooling ourselves and realize we are the answer to this problem. I know it could be hard to change our way of thinking but we must try with everything that is within us. That the sins of apartheid will be stopped and people will rise up out of the system and set in place a new standard in our homes and neighborhoods we can change things. We must become an instrument of change. Start with yourself and work outward acknowledge that we can start new habits. Remember a habit begins when we have the knowledge to do, and know what to do and can see the benefits of doing we can start today. Don't put it off start where you are. I know that there are things in our past that stop us: sometimes we don't even know why. We can get ahead, however, we must look back and deal with some of these things so we can break free. I think the most difficult time in my life was when I was about 8 or 9. Someone I trusted sexually abused me. While it was happening I used to imagine I was somewhere else to escape the pain and embarrassment. I became very withdrawn and started to act out in school and home. I even thought of acting out the same thing out on a younger friend of mine. But I thought about the pain I felt and did not want anyone to feel that pain. When I was about 11 it happened again with a friend of the family I trusted. This person, really let me down and hurt me.

I used to wish that person were dead and even planned on how I was going to kill them sometime at night. I would cry all night thinking it was my fault. I began to hate myself and I began to act it out, I would have sex with anyone I could. It became a part of me because I kept it to myself and did not tell anyone. I had hate in my heart and I wanted to hurt as many people as I could. It's true that hurt people hurt people. So if someone hurts you in most cases they were hurt too. That is why it is so important to release and forgive so you won't retain the sins of people that hurt you and start acting out the same things. It is also true you become what you hate and like the one you hate. Hate and lust are related, they travel together and eat away at you until it consumes you. It is very hard to brake free.

So who am I?

I am God friend, a believer in the gospel of Jesus Christ, a window of heaven, an interment of change, a prayer warrior, more than a conqueror, an overcomer. And I am set free by the blood of the Lamb of God……………..

Chapter #4 is it my fault?

Because any sex sin goes very deep inside you to the sub level of your mind and take root and grows it is so important to not think it is your fault. Imagine being 8 years old and being painfully sexually abused and not telling anyone. [Hate it but blaming yourself for it. Help is only a call or being too ashamed to tell someone.] And living with this secret all the time. There are some signs of sexual abuse you can look for like:

1. Not being able to look someone in the eyes. There are some kids that are natural shy so just watch the child.

2. Withdrawn and very quite. A child who will not ask for help even if he/she is in pain.

3. A child that never complains about anything. Most kids are natural complainer. When a child never complains take note.

4. A child who is a loner. Likes to be alone and prefers to stay at home instead of playing outside with friends

5. A lack of self-respect or self-worth is a big sign.

Just remember this is never your fault when someone hurts you. You are the victim but you do not have to stay there. There is a way out.

You need to seek help a Christian counselor or a friend, the important thing is to tell someone about what happen to you and don't keep it to yourself. Also you must find it in your heart to forgive them, not for them but for you. This will set you free...

Chapter #5 Getting Free

[Getting free has to take place in the mind you must tell someone what happened to you and then try to forgive the person who did wrong to you.] [Not forget but forgive.] The best way to do this is to start to see that person as someone that was hurt too. Pray for healing to take place. You can't hate someone you pray for everyday. Freeing your mind is hard but faith comes by hearing things over and over again. That is why it is so important to speak to you and say good uplifting things. Write it down make a confession and say it every day and you will believe it after you have heard it over and over again. The biggest thing that stops men and woman are what they see.

We must try to overcome the senses and remember we are over comers, and more than conquerors. You must let the principles in the word of God get into your spirit and free you. The bibles say and the truth will set people free. We need to hang out with people who make you uncomfortable that make you think and grow. Relying on God and his word. Here are some confessions:

1. I can do all things through Christ who gives me power.
2. I have what it takes to make it.
3. All things work together for we who love the lord

Your freedom depends on the time you spend thinking and doing something to get free. I remember a story about some people who were slaves for a long time and after some time they became free. In the first stage of their freedom is the hardest. Because you were a slave you did not have to think. All you had to do is what you were told to do. But now you have to think and make decisions on your own. To some people this is terrifying because most people like to be lead around, just look at the fashion industry and you can see in the hood all the young men look the same.

They take jail fashion and think it is hot. The saggy look came from jail because you can't have belts in jail. So all the young men dress like prisoners and think it's cool. You see young men walking around with two hundred dollar sneakers and driving nice cars they can't afford to put gas in because the videos says it is cool. Most of the cars and gold are props are rented for the videos and some kid are brain washed into believing that to have these things mean you made it. So we become slaves to the things they control us and keep us in bondage. All our life in debt we can't get out. If we learn to think independently we will be much happier. I told my 15-year-old son and 16-year-old daughter take Christmas for example, everyone is buying gifts and many can't afford it but they feel they must because everyone else is doing it.

I told my children it is God's birthday not yours so I will not buy anything until after Christmas. It makes sense 50% to 70% off don't you think so. Don't do things because everyone is doing it, buy when the timing is right and you can buy more? But this is going against the flow. This is thinking independently, the way to freedom.

Affirmation

_____

_____

_____

_____

_____

Chapter #6 Comfort zone

We all have a circle of influence on the job and in our home and our relationships. It takes courage to get out of the circle. Look at the diagram my zone:

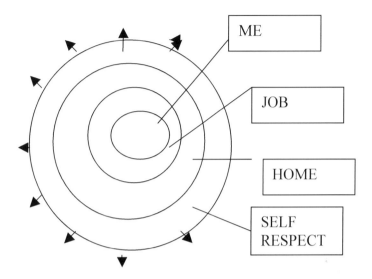

The biggest rewards are outside your comfort zone.

Good	Better or Best God Plains for me
Things in my Zone	**Things outside of my Zone**
Going to church	Teaching in church
Job	Businesses
Renting an Apartment	Owning my homes
Friends	Life Long Partnership
Self Respect	Respect for others and self

In order to get out of your comfort zone you must put it on paper and find out where you are, and how to get to the things outside of your zone. Once you get out, the circle gets bigger and your influences get larger and larger. There are no limits in you. If you reveal your weaknesses and be specific about where you're going, and remind your self-everyday you will see yourself making progress.

In my comfort zone I was safe and outside of it I was very uncomfortable. There are many fears we must deal with. To get out of the zone. I had a fear of reading in front of people because in school I had ADD. Attention Deficit

Disorder and dyslexia that is what they call it. But when I was going to school we called it dumb. And kids would laugh at you and pick on you if you missed words or mixed them up. I would only read what I saw on the page and my mind would mix everything up. But when I got by my self and read, it would be much clearer and the words would come together.

Spelling words was and still is a big challenge for me. Even to this day my spelling is not so good. But I force myself to read in front of people and my fear was still there. But I did not let it stop me from getting ahead. But now before I read in front of people I feel the fear and then I do it anyway. The more you do it the less fear you feel. It has been twenty years since I pushed myself to overcome my fear of reading in front of people. It is still hard but the fear is a part of the process. It will always be there. You must feel the fear ad do it anyway. The fear is not a wall any more. It is more like a door I have to walk through to get to where I am going. That is just one fear I had to over come. There are many more we must take our fears one at a time and confront them and overcome them by asking God to help us to fight the fear. And move out of your comfort zone to your God given Destiny.

Affirmation

_____

_____

_____

_____

_____

Chapter #7 Time Management Zone

4 Part Systems

1# Things that Need to be done now	2# Things that our important to my growth. Working out
3# Things to do for others	4# Things that don't help at all.

In order to get out of a zone you have been in all of your life you must do things different. If you want different results you must do something you never did. You need to spend most of your time in zone #2 if you want to grow ask yourself this question is this making me grow if not find out where you are in this 4 part time zone. And get back to zone #2 let's get an example lets use health. Things in area 1# are in your face.

It is phone call, every day emergency you can get away from them. It is like thing's I must now. Like the baby crying, the problem at work, most people live in this area. They spend all their lives reacting to the things all around them. And this dominates their life. So they do not have time to work out or eat right because they're too busy putting out fires in their lives. Then there are the people in zone 3# who have no boundaries.

They let anyone invade their space. They cannot say no. And they never get things done in their lives because they're always doing for someone else. Then after awhile they run out of gas and burn themselves out because they never take time to put back some of the things they give out so much. Then you have people in zone #4. This zone is filled with destructive things. Things that bring you down destroy and damage you. Like spending time using drugs or on the Internet for hours looking at pornography and like spending time in unhealthy relationships.

This is a pattern for a lot people in the inter city. This is the most powerful zone. The one many get stuck in and cannot get out. It eventually takes your life and destroys your mental state.

To get out of this you need help from God and people who love you. Then there is zone #2.

I am a chef by profession. One day I was training someone in the art of butchering. The person was so ready to learn and started cutting away at the meat, I came back to check on him and he was sweating and had a cut finger and messed up a lot of cuts. I asked him what do you thing you did wrong. He looked at me with sweat dripping down his face and said I did every thing you said. I said to him, everything but sharpened your knife. At the beginning of our training, I told him that his knife is his best friend and to treat it like that.

Because a dull knife makes your work harder and you can cut yourself easier because you have to apply more pressure and you make less mistakes with a sharp knife. It is the same way in life and in zone two. The Things that are foundational to your growing are the things you must take time to do. Like work out, eat right to sharpen your tool, your body. Read every day to sharpen your mind.

Take time at the beginning of your year, month, week, and day to make plans to put some structure in your life so you are not just running around putting out fires, Also things like getting the proper rest. Taking vacations. Also one of the hardest things to do in this world is to learn how to enjoy spending time alone with God. Not doing anything but get a pen and paper and go somewhere you will not be disturbed and listen for instruction, then write it.

This is one of the most valuable things you can do and it takes discipline at first. As soon as you get alone your mind get flooded with thoughts from everywhere. You start to think of all you have to do, and why are you wasting time doing nothing. This thought is as far away from the truth as you can get. This is valuable time in zone #2. Times spent in this setting things start to open up and wisdom pours in because you are taking time to here from God and you get time to sort out the bad thoughts and reinforce the good ones. So remember zones #2 stay there as much as you can..

Zone #1- needs to be done now (baby crying or putting out fire at work must do)

Zone #2-important for growth (Reading, exercise, spending time with God, sharpening the knife time alone

Zone #3- Things you do for others (This is important but you must take time to Put back the things you give out or you will burn out..

Zone #4 – Things that do not help at all (Doing drugs, drinking, in bad relationships)

Remember the part of you that you feed the most will dominate if you feed flesh it will rule and you will be out of control. If you feed the spirit man he will be in control. If you feed the mind it will rule. There must be a balance. Take time to spend in zone 1, 2, 3 Try to spend most o your time in zone 2# and your life will be much more structured and you will get things done and done right. Because you are more balanced so get a piece of paper and make a large box and start to put the things you do in the proper zone. Be conscious of what is going on in your life.

See if you spending time in zone#4 and if so make yourself spend more time in the other 3 zones. Within a week or two you will see your growth and you will be headed in the right direction. Get the book, 7 Habits of Highly Effective people, by Steven Covey and read it. It will change your life and your way of thinking.

Affirmation

_____

_____

_____

_____

_____

Chapter #8 Cause and Effect

The things you do will affect you later. This is the principle of sowing and reaping. This works even if you do not try. It is a law like gravity on earth. You can't get away from it. Living in the city what you see is what you get or is it. Most people are not concerned with effect because they are so wrapped up in their life and the things they want. Never looking at the effects of there actions. Like a young lady meets a man and he looks good. They go out and before you can get to know him you sleep with him. He tells you, you are his first and we don't need protection and you're so in love with him you give in, never thinking about the effects of your actions.

Later you find he had mental problems and has given five girls the Aides virus and your number six and you're pregnant. We must learn to count the cost of our actions and our words. Words are like weapon, they hurt like bullets, and they go deep and do internal damage to the hearts and minds. When I was younger I use to tell women I loved them just to get what I wanted. "I want to spend the rest of my life with you" I would say but in my heart I did not mean it.

Today we do it all the time lying and hurting for our own gain after we get what we want then we leave them. But the girl can't handle it you messed up her mind and she wants to get even. She sees you with someone else and pulls out a gun and shoots you both.

This is not made up stories. This happens every day in the city. People getting killed for saying the wrong things to the wrong person. Let me remind you this is a law. You can't get away from it. What you do will come back to you. What you say can kill and get you killed. So remember cause and effect and have it work for you by doing good things to others. Don't speak death. Speak life, and not lies but the truth and you will receive what you put out. The law of sowing and reaping cause and effect.

Chapter #9 Mental Slavery

What is slavery? It is being limited in the things you can do. Not being able to think for yourself. Having restrictions on you so that your movement is limited to someone else's thoughts of what you can do not your own. This is the state of most people. A man or woman cannot go beyond their ability to think. If his ability to think is being controlled, they are enslaved. In today's world the chains are not on our legs and arms but on our minds. Most of us are slaves and don't even know it. That's the sad part, we are being told what to wear, what to think, and how to live. There is no freedom, when most of your choices are taken away. As I said before, I was born and raised in Paterson and I believe that all cities have certain spirits in control over them.

In Paterson, the spirit of oppression and the spirit of division and suppression. These are the main three spirits that rule here. The people in the inner city can't control their life. Also there are other spirits that travel with these spirits like depression, addictions, low self-esteem and apathy. With this combination it is hard to shake. These spirits have strong holds in this city and others. A strong hold is when these spirits have been ruling so long that you do not even think something is wrong. People living on the streets, drug dealers all over the city, prostitutes walking all over the city and kids as young as nine or ten using, selling drugs. To have a school system were more are dropping out then staying in school is a crime itself. When I see our libraries closing and liquor stores opening in its place, and no one is stopping this it is a strong hold on the city.

There is something holding you that you can't see and you don't know it there. It's a spirit of oppression and depression, along with being treated unfairly. There are people who work here that will never live here because they see what is happening this is a warning. The spirit of division to divide and conquer it is a war strategy used by military all over the world and is also use in the inner city to keep someone under control. It works and has been used for thousands of years. It is legal just like suppression. This spirit is the one that is used to hold you down. You find it in the schools and in the government in the city.

In Paterson it has been going on for years and no one has stopped it. It was so bad that the state had to take over the public schools. Let us start there. The schools are not set up for you to learn life skills and how to live in the hood. The classes were too crowded. And most of the kids could not keep up with the lesson plans. Because they were time sensitive. They have to teach a certain amount of lessons by a certain time. If you did not get the work, you got left behind and it would go on for years. So you are in school being frustrated and then behavior problems start because you would rather be looked at as bad then dumb. In school I was one of these children.

I remember in school the teacher asking me to read out aloud. I tried it and I kept saying words that were not on the page, mixing my words up and getting stuck on small words. The other kids would make fun of me. It was a lot of kids in my class that could not read. In the fourth grade I remember bringing home a report card with seven F's and 6 D's and one B in gym I was failing all my classes and I needed help, however my teacher could not slow down the work.so I could catch up. By the fourth marking period I had all D's.

My teacher told my mom I was trying so they gave me a D that was passing so I never got left back. Even though I did not understand a lot of the work, I was pushed through the system. When I was in the eleventh grade in Eastside High School, you must know of this school, it was in a movie called "Lean on me". It was a school out of control. A man name Joe Clark save hundreds of kids from dropping out of school. The drop out rate was still 50 to 60 percent of Black and Hispanic males. The suppressed school system is still going on. Back in slavery times the master would try to keep the slaves form reading. Reading was a crime and you were punished if you were caught reading. Today it is a crime if you don't read you get punished.

I encourage young Black men and all men to read all the time. Knowledge can be given but cannot be taken away. Slavery is still going on. A lot of it is built into today's every day life. You must be aware it is here and try with everything that is in you not to be a part of the system. There are many young men in jail, in homeless shelters or in the cemeteries because of the system. The Bible says we do not fight flesh and blood but a system that was set up by the enemy of our soul.

The divider is one who uses people to hate and to neglect other people. It is wrong to think that the white man has done this to you. It is part of a plan to keep you down. Satan is the one who leads it he comes to kill, steal and destroy. That is his job it is our job to fight back anyway we can. The weapons we use to hurt other men are wrong. We need new weapons like wisdom, knowledge, understanding and education. These weapons are lasting and can be taught to your children and their children. When I was in Eastside High School, it was out of control. We were being suppressed in every area of our life. Then came a man name Clark. He was not a part of the system and he changed things for a while. However, when you go against the system you're not liked, and people become scared because the system is not in place and you are free to do something about your situation it is scary and uncomfortable and change is even more frightening to some people, so they said, he had to go.

I was there before he came and we could do whatever we wanted in school. The Bathrooms were drugs and cigarette dens and it was so many people in the bathroom getting high. No one got in trouble some time we used to sit in the café all day. No one would say anything to us. We would go to the pool hall and get high all day and it was hundreds of kids out there and the police would ride by and let us keep doing our dirt.

Drinking and getting high was a norm, and I did not want to go in the school because by this time in high school, my schoolwork was completely behind. I was not trying. I remember missing 87 days out of school and the school never called and there was no cut office in the school .so I said we could do what we wanted. It was three guys I used to be with, my brother Tony, Kenny Black, and Lee Savage and we called ourselves "The Force" like star wars. We loved to party and get high. We did all kinds of drugs, acid, misculin, cocaine, p-dope. I am surprised we did not die. We thought we were having fun but it was killing us. Everyone was doing it. It was the "in thing.' We were slaves and did not know it at the age 16 ½ my brother and I moved out of my mother's house. We had fake ID's and got jobs working with men. We got our own apartment on Graham Avenue.

It was all out of control, the sex, drugs and alcohol. My mom told us if you can't obey my rules you have to go so we went. Sometimes you can be in a place in our lives that it does not make any sense and still just go along with it. Why? Because a lot of time all our decisions are being made for us by our surroundings. We as a people must learn how to make our own decisions and stop following the flow and learn to think on our own. For hundreds of years we have been taught how to think in the system. There are many of us that are trapped by there thoughts and can't get free.

Let me help you with this profound statement – WAKE UP! Stop being lead and be a leader. Make plans to get out of the mindset that you have to fit in. The people that fit in are followers. The ones that do not are leaders. You don't have to change everything about you at once. Start with the way you think. Begin with the end in mind. Think about where you want to go in life in the future. Then look at your actions and see if your actions will take you there. If not then change a little at a time. Start to read about where you are going. Get all the books you can on the subject and fill your mind with the thoughts of being there and doing these things until it is so real you can taste it. Slowly you will start moving in the right direction. If you can believe it you can achieve it. This statement is true and is a principle for change.

I remember being in high school and having my own apartment. I was 16 ½ and my brother was 15. We moved out of mom's house it was wild. We only went to school when we wanted to, which weren't often. Eventually we just dropped out. My brother and I got full time jobs and became workingmen. My first real job was as a dishwasher and prep cook. My brother did the same. I thank God for my mom. She taught us to work around the house. We would do anything to make a little money.

Me, and my brothers Beasley, Luther, Michael used to work in supermarkets overnight waxing floors with my mom's friend, Mr. Jimmy. Mr. Jimmy taught us to work hard to get what we wanted. He would say, "if you want it, work for it" and that suck with us. Even though we worked hard we were not around Mr. Jimmy all the time but we had to go back into the system. The system had failed us. The biggest enemy was not being black and poor but it was the way we were trained to think by the system. After dropping out of high school in the 11th grade and could only read at a 3rd grade level, looking back I see how I was pushed through school and not taught anything.

Thousands of kids just like me just dropped out. I think the drop out rate was about 50 to 60 % for black males. That in itself was a crime and someone should pay for it. I guess they said if we don't teach them, we can control them. A man cannot go beyond his ability to comprehend. So instead of teaching us they put us in jails and treated us like animals. The only thing that saved me, and my brothers from a life of jail was having a hard working foundation in our lives. This is the questions, is it our fault or was it set up for me to fail?

How can a young man in this kind of environment make it, very few did? In order to survive we had to become part of a gang. The name of our gang was the young dragons. It was a karate gang. To get into the gang you had to walk the hall of pain. The hall of pain was when all the members would line up in 2 lines and you had to walk through the middle with your hands at your sides and everyone would get to hit you as hard as they could and you could not cry. When you came through the hall of pain you knew why they called it that. The next thing you had to do was to take a dare. One of the leaders in the gang would pick a dangerous act and you would be dared to do it. I remember one of my good friends I will call him Bill to protect his family. He took a dare the elevator jump. We lived in the projects and the building each had 15 floors. When we got to the 15th floor we would climb on top of the elevators and jump from one to the other while it was moving.

My friend bill wanted to get into the gang so bad he took the dare. When he jumped his coat got caught in one of the elevators and he was crushed between two elevators and his head was crushed. I remember watching them taking him out. There was so much blood I could not see his face. That evening all the gang members got together to drink Wild Irish Rose. They poured a little out for Bill the brother who is no longer here. There were about 20 guys in our gang. Out of them only 2 are alive today. Thank God I am one of them. What made me get out of the gang was when my mom and dad who were divorced for 10 years remarried. They moved us out of the projects. I believe that saved my life. I believed that slavery is still going on and even as an adult you can still be a victim of it. Very few made it out. However, there is a way out. That way is to think out of the box.

To understand, that our real enemy is our way of thinking. If we could open our minds and see ourselves and where we are and find a direction of where to go doors will open up all around us. It would be like a man who's lost all his life and someone gives him a map and clear directions on how to get to his destination. When we wander through life with no aim we will miss it all the time. We need to change the way we do things. We don't need to change our whole life at once, just change today, or this hour, or this minute. Little changes everyday will put you on a path to change. And before you know it your life is different. You will see the fruit of change come into your life. It's time to listen more to the people around you. Listening is a powerful skill. It takes a lot to really listen. If you hear something that moves you in the right direction put it to use.

But when you listen make sure the person has wisdom or more knowledge than you.

Start to read any and everything that you get your hands on, especially things that are uplifting, motivating and inspiring. You will be set free. For example, the Bible says faith comes by hearing and hearing over and over again. You must learn to make reading a habit. It has been said to hide something from a black man all you have to do is put it in a book. This is true of black men in the inner city. This must change so we can be free. I have learned to take every chance I get and read and not watch so much TV.

At first it was very hard, however, the rewards are unbelievable. My understanding has grown and my way of thinking has also grown. This is a must do! I can't stress it enough. Next you have to be around people that make you think who to challenge you, and make you quiet. Because of their wisdom and pick their brain ask questions and see how fast you grow.

No question is a dumb question. Many think if you ask questions it makes us look dumb. That is far from the truth. That way of thinking has also enslaved us. You must get started right away. Set a time aside and read everyday. Do it and the chains will come off your mind?

Affirmation

_____

_____

_____

_____

_____

Chapter #10 Improvement through purpose

1. What is purpose: object in view
2. To Aim
3. Effect
4. Intend
5. Determine resolute
6. Why am I here

The late Miles Monroe said, "Death is not a tragedy. What is a tragedy is life without a reason." The most frustrating thing is to have time and not know why. Here are some of the effects of not knowing your purpose:

- Hopelessness
- No self control
- Lack of judgment in all areas
- Attempted suicide
- Low self esteem
- Lack of drive
- Lack of direction
- Drug use and drinking
- Sleeping around (no respect for your body)
- Unfulfilled life without meaning

How to find our purpose? In order to find our purpose we have to go to the source – God. He made us and knows all about us. He gave us a book of instructions on how we work and are maintained. So therefore when we read this book and follow its principles, things will always turn out the way it was written. For example, James 1:25, if a man looks closely into the perfect law that set men free and keeps on paying attention to it and dose not simply listen and forget it but put it into practice, that person will be blessed in all things.

Another way we find out our purpose is in worship. As we worship, if it is true worship is done in the spirit. For we as men truly get into a worship state of mind. We have to get into the presence of God. Often I'm lying before the Lord and praying and being sensitive and sometime just being quiet and listening for his voice that comes from the inside out. Satin always work from the outside in. Satan works through our senses. God is always speaking to us all the time giving us direction and guidance. But most of the time we are too busy to hear to make your spirit more alert you must do spiritual exercises. Like fasting and meditating on the word. Meditation is not spooky but it is getting the word of God and saying it over and over or thinking about it all day. Isaiah 59:6 say "This kind of fasting I want is to remove the chains of oppression, which is satin's attempt to stop you from getting closer to God and to stop you from getting closer to God and to stop you from hearing him and letting him guide you to reach your purpose. Isaiah 59:7 it will remove the yoke of injustice and let the oppressed go free. Because most of us are in bondage to something and all are in bondage to the flesh. We need to put the flesh under control so we can hear from God through our spirits.

When we do this by fasting and praying and meditation on God's word we are something that enriches our spirit man when we read books about God and the spirit of God by doing this our spirit man will become strong and give us the power through God to shake off oppression and be free.

So we can take back what the devil has stolen from us. After a while of doing this it will become a habit and we will become washed with the water of the Word of God. Man is a three part being. The first part is the spirit man. This part joins together with God after we are born again we become a part of his son, Jesus Christ, joint heirs to God's Kingdom. With all the rights of the King's Kids everything is available to us in God's kingdom. By our spirit man we can be lead in the right and wrong ways to go. Also this is the only part of a man that can truly worship God and have fellowship with him. This part of you cannot be destroyed. This part cannot die and well live-forever. You chose where you would spend eternity by the choices you make in your life. To live for God, is to die to self.

The spirit man is so much like God our Father and should be in control of the whole man. However in most cases it is not. The second part of man is emotions or intellect and feeling or the mind. The mind and the spirit are not the same. Our mind controls our body functions like heart beat movements and all the rest. Our spirit controls our moral life, our direction and conscious. How we relate to God and others. If we did whatever we felt like doing, we would be in big trouble sometimes through thoughts that come into our minds. The thoughts are not good or are unhealthy and could cause us to do harm to ourselves and to others. So our minds and spirits work together.

To give us balance in our lives our God knows what he was doing when he put us together and if we would only take the instruction manual and uses it we would not be in so much trouble or have so much depression or stress in our lives. Our system is crossed and out of whack.

The third man is the flesh. The flesh is the part of man that is controlled by the five senses—taste, touch, smell, sight and hearing. I call them the five gates to hell. If you let this part of you rule that's where you're going—to hell. It has no control; it is selfish and only wants to please self at all and any cost. For example, your body is not going to heaven or hell it is only going to be buried in the ground. When it dies it will never rise again. So its desire is to get all the pleasure it can while it is here.

The flesh will lead you into pornographic web sites; it will cause you to be enslaved by lust of all kinds. When you start the sin in progress and becomes bigger and bigger and leads to spiritual death. Sometimes after spiritual death, comes death of the body. It will cause you to over eat and eat the wrong things and cause sickness to your body. It will control you if you let it and so it will be out control and the things you do will be all fleshly controlled. This is a dangerous place to be. It will cause you to drink and use drugs and all kinds of ungodly things like have sex with animals or dead people or kids.

Also, same sex relationships or with prostitutes with unprotected sex. This part of us we have to put under control often by fasting and praying. Also making the bodies do what it does not want to do like praise God or pray. Exercise and eat right when you do these things your life will change and you will grow in the mind and spirit. When the flesh is under submission we can hear from God more clearly and move on what he says to us about our purpose.

How to hear his voice: It is good to know how God speaks to you. He speaks in many ways. One-way is a still small voice that comes from the inside of you. You must be quiet and willing to position yourself to listen in faith expecting to hear from him. Get a paper and pen and wait for instruction. You must believe without a doubt God will speak to you. Be ready to receive from the Holy Spirit. If you sit quiet long enough words will start to come to your mind, not your thoughts, your thoughts are self - centered—God's thoughts are for the body of Christ and will benefit all, you included. Fasting plays a big roll in the clarity of God's voice. You are more sensitive to God and the things around you and people around you. Read Isaiah 58:6 on fasting.

Another way to hear from him is through others. God uses other people to bring blessing into our lives. It is a verse in the Bible that says that God will open up the windows of Heaven and pour you out Blessings. This means God uses people, his people as instruments of blessings to help and bless the body. He works through his people in all he does on earth. We are in God's hands, eyes, ears mouth, and when God, man or woman have this knowledge and act upon it their lives and all around them will be changed - why because God is at work in them.

Affirmation

_____

_____

_____

_____

_____

Chapter #11 Power Points of Change

Most people are afraid of change because they can't control what happens next. They must rely on faith in their decisions. So they don't make any. That will be too uncomfortable. They stay where they are hoping change will come to them and all around them. I believe God is the author of change and that every thing must change if it does not something is wrong with it. Here are some power points of change. Say them to yourself over and over until you believe it and live them.

FAITH

1. Poverty and Riches are both well springs of faith your choice.
2. You can change the direction of your faith and move in a direction you believe
3. Faith is indispensable for your success faith is strengthened by instruction you give your subconscious mind.
4. You can't think yourself into disaster or victory and happiness in the same circumstance its your choice.
5. Thoughts can attract related thoughts making a million minds work as one mind.
6. You must be willing to give before you get this will not change.
7. There are no limitations to the mind except those we acknowledge.

DESIRE

A state of mind that can put you in a position to do the impossible; if used in a bad way can destroy you.

1. When desire focuses great force toward your victory you never need to retreat.
2. Desire builds new victories out of temporary defeats.
3. Temporary defeats a loss of a battle but the war is still going on – it's not over.
4. A man who the doctor expected to die within weeks but desire to live and does. It works.

Thoughts are vehicles of change:

The way you think is your only limitations. A man cannot grow beyond his ability to think. There are many physical barriers that stand in ones way. But these can be climbed over, under or even walked around but the chains in the mind can only be removed by first opening ones mind to change. To change ones train of thought. What you're thinking is where you are going. Your thoughts are vehicles of change. So train your mind and speak to yourself good things like:

1. What ever the mind can conceive and believe it can achieve.
2. There is nothing impossible.
3. In your weakness God is made strong if you trust him.
4. F-E-A-R   F – False   E – Evidence   A – Appearing   R – Real
5. You can transmit your faith and persistence to others to get the impossible done well.
6. Control your thoughts, asks yourself the right questions.
7. Don't give up – your blessings could be right in front of you.

Let me take these seven thoughts and bring life to them.

Whatever the mind can conceive and believe it can achieve. Growing up in the hood has a way of making you think certain ways. I use to think what I heard every day, what my mom would tell me and teacher and others like friends. A teacher told me one day, "you are a bum, and you will never be anything."

For years her words stuck to me and I thought in that way. Words are powerful and are like deadly weapons to your thoughts. But, as I got a little older someone once said to me, "if you work hard, you can get what ever you want. So that became my thought process and I began to go after what I wanted by working hard. After a while, I was told working hard is one thing but working smart is the way to go. So my paradyne shifted again. There is a way to protect your mind from others views words as things not just words but gifts, [some bad and some you have the power to escape] the gift or refuse it. It is your choice. If someone gives you some (bad gifts) you can refuse them and the gifts still belongs to the giver. Instead of rejecting these thoughts, you begin to own them and they become yours. They become a part of how you think, and this is a big problem.

We stumble over all the words that are being spoken to us and stop our progress in life. I tell my children if you can imagine something there is a way to do it. You have to find the way. It's your job, and with God's help you can do it.

I also would tell them if they were having problems in school. First you must believe you can do it and if you do that half the battle is won. Then you have to study and be proactive if your teacher tells you to work on chapter one, do chapters 2 and 3 too. Why, it gives you a head start. and not only can you keep up but you can lead the class and everyone will think you are smart. But you were just proactive. If you have problems taking test like a lot of us, before you start close your eyes and use your imagination. See your paper in front of you, when you see it, see an "A" at the top of the page. Then ask God to help you remember all you have studied and to give you total recall of your work. It could work for you. Whatever the mind can conceive and believe it can achieve.

This is a true statement. There are many things we thought was impossible: a man on the moon, cell phones, the Internet, etc. If you look around you will see someone made it possible. They believed and did not stop until they made it happen. So the things we think are impossible are opportunities for God to show him self strong. All He needs is someone to believe and act on what they believe. What is in line with God's word and watch him work through your faith.

In your weakness God is made strong.

God uses our time of weakness to show his truth. There are many stories in the Bible where God mad the impossible happen. In the time of weakness, we can be like Gideon where he used 300 against 300,000. David and Goliath, Daniel in the Lion's Den and many, many more. God is in control and sometime when we get victory we forget where it came from. In the impossible situation we do not know how it happens. God made a way in a no way situation the word of God says God is seeking someone who he can show himself strong through that when you trust in God, everyone knows it. He will not let you down because He cannot lie. If His word says it, it will be done. You can take it to the bank. I am not going to use big words to impress you, or my knowledge of the Word. What I know is true, and God never fails. Show him your weakness and he will give you strength. If you trust him do not let fear stop you. What is fear: here is a modifier the describes it:

F-E-A-R

False
Evidence
Appearing
Real

The things that keep us from achieving our goals are fear. There are all kinds of fear. Some call them phobias. The Bible says that perfect love cast out all fear. If we learn to use God's word as a guide we can make our life much better.

Affirmation

_____

_____

_____

_____

_____

Chapter # 12 The Principles of Christ (When he started His ministry)

The first thing Jesus said was repent!!! For the kingdom of God is at hand. It took me awhile to understand this. I thought it to mean God was coming back soon but it meant something totally different. The meaning was the kingdom of God is here now; it is close to you. You can reach out and touch it with your hand or your heart. The kingdom is God's way of doing things. When Jesus came to earth to show us the kingdom and to teach us the principles to live in the kingdom. The Bible says we will be transformed by the renewing of our minds. In the gospel, Jesus taught about all kinds of things related to the kingdom and this is my interpretation of what he taught his disciples about the kingdom.

The first step –open the door to the kingdom

Repenting is the foundational part of the kingdom principles. There are two parts to repentance. The first is being sorry. Heart felt sorry for the things you have done. You know you have displeased God and acknowledge all he has done for you. He gave his life for your sins. Take time to really think about what you did and the pain it caused to you and to others. Ask for forgiveness, heartfelt forgiveness from God and also the people involved in the hurt.

The next part is a change of direction. Change the way you live and do things. If you do both of these things together, you will experience true repentance. If you were self-centered, become Christ centered. Find your sin and turn from it, run from it as far as you can in the other direction. This is true repentance. This is what Jesus taught.

Understanding The Kingdom

The kingdom of God is the Word of God put into action. It's a system where the Word of God rules over all things in your life. If we read the Word of God and learn what it says about everything in our life and live by that word, we will be living in the Kingdom of God. A total submission to God is what He wants. It takes work but it can be done by faith. You must speak the Word out loud over and over. Meditate on the Word day and night until it becomes a part of you.

The Bible says faith comes by hearing and hearing by the Word of God. This is the principle to changing anything in your life. You must hear it until you believe it and then and only then you will act on it.

Come follow me

After Jesus taught the Word to the disciples and they believed it, he challenged them to do as he did and follow him. The disciples had to give up their old way of thinking and get a new way-God's way. Some disciples had to give up money, the family business, and all they had done until that point in their life to start a new life in the kingdom of God. By following Jesus the way the truth and the light no man can get to the Father except by Him. This is also a life principle. To get the things you never had, you have to do the things you never did in ways you've never done them – this is God's way.

Fishers of Men

Jesus said to them "If you follow me I will make you fishers of men." How do we fish for men? What do we use as bait? The truth is the bait. When man has a little taste of His bait he will want more and soon he will tell other men and they will come to know the truth. The truth will set them free. This is God's way of doing things-by enlightening men to truth, teaching to plant seeds in the lives of others, seeds of the truth, the gospel of Jesus Christ.

Signs and Wonders

After teaching them the truth signs and wonders and miracles began to happen because of faith in the Word sickness left, bad spirits left and lives were transformed. Every time the truth is spoken and believed God can work without anything stopping him. You are open to hear from Him and you can receive healing body and mind and soul – it works. There was a story in the Bible when a little girl had died and Jesus had to clear the room of unbelief in order to bring her back to life. Faith in God's Word has the power to bring you back to life not just ordinary life but the God kind of life (Zoe) a life of principles that work.

How to Be Blessed

Jesus began to teach them the foundations of the word. How you can be blessed. What is blessed a lot of people think it means getting things. Things are only a small part of blessed living.

Blessing is living kingdom principles and reserving God's power to help yourself and others. You can find this teaching in the book of Matthew starting at chapter five verses 3. The Beatitudes. Below I will put them in a chart form:

Blessed if you do this	The Worldly Values	God's Rewards of obedience	How to get there in Gods word
1. Blessed are you that is poor in spirit	Prideful and independent	There is the kingdom of God	James 4:7-10
2. Blessed are those who mourn	Happiness at any cost	God will comfort him	Psalms 51
3. Blessed are the meek	Power hungry people	He will inherit the earth	Matthew 11: 7-30
4. Blessed are those who hunger and thirst for right standing with God	Pursuing personal needs only	He will be filled	John 16: 5:11 Philippians
5. Blessed are the merciful	Strength without feeling	You will be shown mercy	Ephesians 5:1,2
6. Blessed are the poor in heart	The worlds Deception is acceptable	He will see God	1 John 3:1-3
7. Blessed are the peace makers	Think about your own peace and being and no one else's.	God will call you His son	Romans 12:19-21
8. Blessed are the ones who are prosecuted	Weak commitment people	Inherit the kingdom of heaven	2 Timothy 3:12

Follow the word of God in these areas and see the fulfillment of God in your life. In other words, having a blessed life. Get the scripture in your head and heart, say it over and over until it is a part of the way you think. Faith comes by hearing so it must be an ongoing thing. The word of truth is a direct contradiction of society. Typical way of life, Jesus even points out that serious effort to develop these traits is bound to create opposition.

The best example of each trait is found in Jesus himself. If our goal is to become like him, the beatitudes will challenge the way we live each day. Follow Jesus principles. In the gospels no man can dispute these principles. They have been tried and tested for over 2,000 years. In my own life over 30 years it works.

Affirmation

_____

_____

_____

_____

_____

Chapter # 13 The Power of Principles

What is a principle – a fundamental truth or law: a moral rule: the foundation of truth from the pass. It's a Word that gives direction like the principle of a school. The RULES that never change, and a solid map for good and evil. Life's lesson, Principles are not tough, as we should any more. Even in the church they have been watered down and dismissed as out of date. The United States of America was founded on principles from the Word of God. Every wise saying you hear people say can be traced back to God's Word. For He God), is the principal of all principles.

The foundation of life and all we see and know, all of what we see in the word is not an accident but part of a plan of God. Every thing is governed by principles and always will be. People who go against principles go against God himself. In the beginning God made man and woman – why to procreate and to replenish the earth. Even if you don't believe in God you know all animals on earth have a male and female species. To be a homosexual is against God's law and principles. When people start to do what feels good and not what right. This is what's called moral decay. We see it all over our world. We see men and women get married to the same sex. This is wrong and it is not seen as wrong. In these last days there is no right or wrong. A world without right or wrong is a world out of control, which will lead to destruction. This is a principle. It's been seen by the past society when we don't follow principles we will destroy ourselves.

I know a lot of people will disagree with me, but I must warn them of their actions. Principles can help us in all areas of our lives. There is a principle for everything in the teachings of Christ Jesus. He came to show us the way. I read the Bible and also other religious books and all the principles are the same. Everyone agrees with the principles just not with who said the principles, the Son of God. Here is a principle that was hard for me to understand. The principle of love, it is the center of all things. The most powerful weapon in the word, Love. If you use it in every area, you will always win. This is a thing called tough love sometimes you must do what is best for someone and not what makes us comfortable.

For instance, if my brother is on crack and is stealing from me and does not want to get help, using the principle love can be putting him out so he can come to himself and seek help. There is also love, what is best not what is comfortable. Love can change anything and undo any wrong. It may take time but it is a principle that will work. Here is another principle – seedtime in harvest – What you want in life – start to plant in others lives. It you want to receive money, give it away. If you want love, give love away. If you want peace, give peace away. If you want pain, give pain away. If you want forgiveness, give forgiveness away. What you sow you will reap.

You must be very careful where you plant. Make sue it is good ground or someone who will deserve what you give or need it. Don't give pearls to the pigs, they will just step on them and misuse them. We have the principles before us. It will change you – take one month to look at the teaching of Christ and if it does not change you then go back to the way you were.

Not only read the Word, but also meditate on it for 30 days, day and night. You will see the change in your life it is a principle that works! This principle set men free. The word also says if you abide in me, and my Word in you, you can ask what you will and it will be given to you. We only need to get the promises in our hearts and head and act on them.

Affirmation

_____

_____

_____

_____

_____

Chapter #14 what is believing - the Elements of Prayer - (Benefits of Prayer-My daily Prayer-Family Mission Confession)

Believing it is an action word a verb. To do and believe are the same thing. You cannot do something unless you believe it. I heard a story about a little boy who was trapped on the second floor of his house because there was a fire on the first floor. He ran to his door and touched the door knob and it was hot. He ran to the window and looked out and there he saw a big strong man outside. The man held his arms out and said jump. He saw the man was strong and he could catch him if he jumped, but he really didn't believe until he actually jumped. We have to get to a point in our walk with God that we are willing to jump and believe God is strong enough to catch us. Our faith in His Word must come to a point that what he says I will do. So you can't say you believe and not do anything because then you become a liar or you believe there is a God but you deny his power to help you or to save you. God wants us to be true believers and reap the benefits of this Word and live a life from faith to faith and glory to glory. Being an over-comer and more than a concorer in Christ Jesus. We can be if we believe.

The Element of Effective Prayer

1. Repent of all sins and ask God to forgive you. This is so important because it clears the way between you and God – true repentance. Remove all the stuff the stops you from receiving from God and God from receiving from you.

2. Praise: Praise stills the enemy. He cannot operate in the presents of real praise that is done in the spirit with a repented heart and a mind full of thanksgiving opens you up for God's power to come in and stop any distractions of the enemy.

3. Thanksgiving: The prayer of thanksgiving reminds you of all God has done in your life. His faithfulness. It would be a good idea to get a pen and paper and write it down – all he has done and is doing now. Remember the details like the air you breathe and health in your body. When you pray start at the top of your list and state everything. This will open your heart to God even more.

4. Be very specific about praying: Be specific about what you pray about. All your situations write your prayers on paper and state them in detail. Then test them against God's Word. They must be in line with the Word of God in order to be effective. Check them off as God answers them one by one. Keep this notebook you write this in and use it as a history of his faithfulness. He never fails; all of his promises are yes and amen.

5. Put some feet to your prayers: Put it into action. Believe it is already done and move in the direction of the prayer. For example, if you ask God for a business, start getting ready for it. Get the necessary training, talk with people who have already established a business and write down your progress. You will begin to see yourself moving closer to your prayer and watch it unfold before your eyes. When you pray, if it lines up with God's Word, he does it when you pray. Then God has to get you ready for what he already has done for you. So step out in faith and believe you have what you asked for and never doubt. You have it and it will manifest. God loves you and wants you to be blessed but you have to do something. Put feet to your prayers.

The Benefits of Effective Prayer

1. It includes God in all your plans and prepares your heart and mind to give God room to work in your life and when God works things get done.
2. It puts expected results in good hands – there is no stress only trust.
3. It helps you express your anger to God but also, allows you to turn it over to God and he will carry your burden.
4. It shows trust in God even while taking the necessary precautions.
5. It shows your reliance on God for emotional and mental stability.
6. It takes away the compulsion to take revenge and entrusts justice to God.
7. It keeps clear in your mind your own motives for the action in your life.
8. It empowers you for your purpose and builds you up every day.
9. It allows you to get sin off your back by repenting daily of the sin in your life – it lightens the load.

10. It is a form of refuge in times of trouble, a strong tower, the righteous run in and they are safe.

My Daily Prayer – A model prayer

1. I start out by giving thanks and praise for the Word says we enter his gate with thanks giving and then into His courts with praise.

2. The prayer of repentance of my sins of omission and of commission are the sins I know and don't know 1John 1:9.

3. Phil 4: 6-7 I thank Him for all he has done. Very specific and detail and remind Him of His word Matthew 18:18. What we bind on earth he will bind in heaven and what we lose on earth he will lose in heaven. (a) I bind the hand of the enemy (b) Bind thoughts that are not in line with the word that they will not have influence on my actions (c) I lose good ideals (d) I lose favor in my life and my children lives.

4. 2 Cor 10:4,5 I thank God that the weapons of our warfare are to destroy all lies and that they will pull down every obstacle that comes against the knowledge of God. Take every though captive and it must obey Christ. By speaking this every day faith is being made strong.

5. I then pray the prayer of agreement Matt 18:19 if any two come together and agree in his name it shall be done. Then I stand in agreement with the spirit of God. Use His Word then I make a list: (a) we have no lack (b) I am a lender and not a borrower (c) I am an over-comer and more than a concuquer and so on. You can make the list as long as you want.

6. I thank God for the Spiritual Gifts;
   First the power gifts:
   A. Gift of healing
   B. Faith
   C. Miracles
   These are gifts that do something

   The gifts that say something;
   A. Tongues

B. Interpretation of tongues
C. Prophecies

The gift that Reveal something;
a. The word of wisdom
b. The word of knowledge
c. Discerning of spirits

I thank God that these gifts will be given to me as the spirit will and at the times I need them and I will not be afraid to use them for His glory.

I speak the things that be not as if they were. I make a list of all the things I'm believing in God for my life, and my families lives for example:

1. I thank you Lord that I will be a full time worker for you and speak to thousands of people about you.
2. That I am a window of heaven that blessings are poured out of and many will be blessed by what you put in my life.
3. That I have ten million in assets for God to us as He wills.
4. That God owns many businesses through me and they are all prosperous.
5. That no sickness or disease will be able to dwell in my body and my children's bodies.
6. That there is peace in my home and my relationships are blessed with my wife and children.
7. For total recall of the word and so on make the list as long as you like.
8. Then I pray for the pastor of my church and all churches – that Jesus is Lord over them.
9. Then the world leaders and local leaders.
10. Then for boldness to do God's will and speak what he give me.
11. Thank God for the full armor of the Lord:
    a. The Helmet of Salvation
    b. Sword of the Spirit
    c. Breast plate of Righteousness
    d. The Belt of Truth
    e. Shoe of readiness to talk for him
    f. The shield of faith
12. This is a must if you are going to do battle for God. It must be done every day for protection against the wiles of the enemy.

13. I pray that God will use me to bring souls in the kingdom by the hundreds of thousands and they will have a hunger and a thirst for right standing in God.

Family Mission Statement (a model you make your own to fit your family)

"We thank you Father God that this family is a family that stands for truth, unity, compassion for others, love, loyalty. We thank you Father that our foot steps are ordered by the Lord and all our decisions are in line with your Word; that everything we set our hands to do will prosper. We thank you Lord that we are a family that listens to each others opinions; are proactive in all we do; that our attitudes is in line with your word; we focus on the first things first and finish them. Father we put our lives in your hands Lord and we ask for direction. Let your perfect will be done in our lives. You said in your Word if we delight ourselves in You, that You would give us the desires of our heart. So we believe that every bill is paid and every dept is satisfied and that our lives are a witness of your power in work. We thank You no sickness and disease can dwell in our bodies and that all generation curses are broken and never to return again; and we bind every contrary spirit in Jesus' name that it will not be able to influence us in any way. Father help us to live these words and to abide in your Word in this generation and the generations to come in Jesus' name Amen."

Chapter # 15 Money

This is a very important topic. It is a topic that is very sensitive to folk. To some it makes them uncomfortable and others it controls there every thought and decision. In the hood we use it to buy bling, bling or gold, cars, diamond studs, name brand stuff and to look good for others. In other neighborhoods it is looked at as a tool to create a good future and to get the things that are important like a home, stocks, and bonds, college funds and a better life for their children or an inheritance. In most black communities the only thing that is left for the next generation is bills and clothes, lots of clothes and shoes, maybe a car and the payments to go with it.

As children we were never really taught about money. All we were taught was we did not have enough of it and it doesn't grow on trees. So most of are education about money came from TV and what we saw in the streets. Try to keep up with the Jacksons. Let me give you some of the lessons about money you will never learn in school. Lesson number one is money is not real! Yes, that right, I said it is not real. It is a made up myth. The things you buy with it are not things that will make you happy but they will only make you want more.

Our whole life we have been taught to work for money and it will make you happy. God has given us money for one reason; it is to be a blessing to others. If you look at money in this way it will make you happy. When I said money is not real, I was saying most of our thoughts about money are not real and will lead us in the wrong direction. Working for money we chase money all our lives and it keeps getting away from us because it is not intended to be chased after but it is intended to chase us. Let me show you how.

In Deuteronomy 28:1 -14 gives you the blessings of obeying God. If you fully obey the Lord your God and carefully follow all his commands, the Lord will set you high above all nations on the earth.

All these blessings will come upon you and over take you if you obey the Lord.

1. You will be blessed in the city and blessed in the country.
2. Your children will be blessed and your work.
3. Everything you touch will be blessed.
4. You will be blessed everywhere you go
5. You will be blessed in battle.
6. The lord will bless your money. You will have more than enough and He will multiply what you have and give you land.
7. He will bless your spiritual life.
8. He will bless you name and it will be respected.
9. He will bless your investments
10. Your finances will be so blessed you will become a lender and will borrow from no one.
11. He will bless your position you will be the head. The boss and all your business will prosper.
12. You must follow My Word. Do not stray and go after things, they will come after you.

Affirmation

_____

_____

_____

_____

_____

Then Chapters 15-68 in Deuteronomy; tells you the curses for disobedience. You must read about everything and He talks about money a lot. God takes a part in our money if we do things his way. If we don't, we will become slaves to money and it will always bring you away from God and you will chase money. If you do it God's way it will chase you and over take you. That is God's way. Seed time and harvest principle. What you sow you will reap it in this life. Whatever you desire give it away. Plant seed let me give you a life story. I didn't have enough to pay my bills. So instead, of paying a little, I planted a seed.

Someone in my church needed money and I had just what he or she needed so I planted in good ground. Good ground is if someone needs something do the right thing with the money you give. Do not give to someone who is on drugs or a gambler. This is bad ground and your money will be used for evil and will not bring a return. So make sure you plant it in good ground. God uses people to bless people and the thing He brings into your life is not just for you but you are to share your blessing with others. If you do this on a regular basis, God will bless you with more.

To whom much is given much is required. His goal is to make you a window. Yes that's right, a window. God talks about opening the windows of heaven and pouring out blessings you will not have room to receive. These are not windows in the sky but on earth. People should understand that God owns everything. We are just stewards of the things in our lives. They do not belong to us we are given things for a reason and it is to be a blessing to God's people by planting seed in their lives and expecting a harvest.

The thing about a seed is it has to be planted to grow and watered and fertilized to grow. If you put seeds on top of your dresser or under your bed or in a shoe box it will not grow. You must plant it. It will stay a seed until it is planted and you will not get any reward from it. When you plant, it becomes a plant and then a tree and it brings forth fruit. The benefit of the planting in each fruit is more seeds more opportunity to plant so we should be looking for more opportunity to plant.

When we get this principle inside our spirit and do it all the time like the Word of God says, the blessings will over take us and we will not have enough room to keep the blessings and we will not be able to give it away fast enough. This is the secret of money. Not to work for it and become its slave but to have it work for you and others around you. Be a blessing so you will be blessed. Use this principle on your job. Don't work for money, work for seed because it is never enough. The money you make, but when you make it seed, then a little is more than enough. Our time and if you plant it in the right ground water your seed not with water but with prayer and thank God for the harvest in advance not just 10 times or 20 times but 100 times, the seed and watch it grow. It takes time for a seed to grow into a tree that bears fruit so you must be patient and keep on planting, expecting a return. When God used his son Jesus as a seed and sent Him to earth to be planted into the hearts of all men and women and the ones who accepted him, as Lord and Savior are fruits of his labor. We are to be living the way He was. To be a blessing to all we come in contact with.

This goes against all the worlds teaching but God said he would take the foolish things of the world to confuse the wise. Man's wisdom says hold on to get rich. God's wisdom say let go to be rich. This is why it is so hared for God's people to get what God has for them. They are doing things the world's way and getting worldly results. We have to look at life as if we are from the same mentality. Our jobs are where we get seed we need all kinds of seed for different crops.

Look at the things we need in our life get that seed if it is love. This seed was given to you for free by Christ. If you want love plant it, show love wherever you go. If you plant a lot the harvest will be greater. The bible says if you sow a little you will get a little if you sow a lot you will get a lot...

Affirmation

_____

_____

_____

_____

_____

Chapter #16 Preparing to plant

As a farmer sometimes the ground is not ready to plant you must prepare the ground to receive the seed. Sometimes it must be broken up and raked out the rocks and weeds before you plant. The same way it is with all seed and ground before you plant love in someone. You sometimes have to break away barriers of hurt that someone else planted. You can do this by praying and sometimes fasting for God to open the person's heart to receive love. Sometimes it happens fast and other times it takes a long time to prepare the ground of someone's heart. This is a very important step in planting of any seed. It must not be overlooked. For seed to grow and the harvest to be a good harvest.

If we want to be like Christ, we must look for opportunities to plant seed in the life of others. Some times the best seed is one where you don't let the person or organizations know where it came from. God knows. He says in His Word that we should not let the right hand know what the left hand is doing if you see a need just give from the heart and see God work. There are many thing that you can give money is not the only thing. You have time, prayer, work, many thing are in the house. Choose what you need and give this to someone else and the seed will be planted. God loves you so much that he gave His Son for you. The price he paid is much greater than anything you are willing to give because you can't beat Gods giving. His mercy is ever lasting and His love is forever.

His grace is always more than enough and his forgiveness is on going if you forgive someone who does not deserve it you are doing what God did for you. You do not deserve forgiveness but he said in his word if you admit your sins God is will forgive you of them. Don't try to hide them from God or someone who can help you. Everything you need begins with a seed. Say this over and over again until it is in your spirit any you will start to act on it. Change the way you look at the job you have and the things you do. Try to always plant seed on your job. Do not work for money, work for seed and look for good ground to plant. Be a farmer for God a window of heaven, a channel of blessings that God can use to bless his people. Your life and your finances will be blessed so much that you will not have room enough to keep it.

Your ability to give or plant will increase 10, 20, 1000 times and you life will be full of good things that you're just watching for God. Waiting for opportunity to give it away. God own it all so there is more than enough to give away. Start today. It feels good to. The fastest way to feel god about you is to give. When you give you are operating in the world of the kingdom and not in the world system. The laws are very different and the rewards are different also. The world's rewards are power and things; God's rewards are ever lasting and always come to pass. You can't count on it every time. It is like a heavenly stock market that has great return. It is guaranteed it is a law of God. The law of seedtime and harvest, and it works.

Affirmation

Chapter #17 Assets and Liability:

This is the only thing you have to know about money. What is an asset and what is a liability? An asset is something that adds to your life. There are all kinds of assets, like paper asset, stocks and money, bonds. Then you have solid assets like gold, silver and other metals like coins. You have income-producing asset. Homes you rent out, businesses you own, investments/. The law of money is a simple one: buy assets. In the hood we were taught that liabilities were asset like gold chains, cars, nice shoes, 200-dollar sneakers, clothes and even the house we live in. The bank let you list some of these things as assets but not one of them is. Your home is a liability. It takes money out of your pocket every month. Your car does the same thing.

What is an asset? It is something that adds to your life. If we are talking about money it is something that puts money in your pocket and a liability is something that takes from your life with no return.

I do not understand why they did not teach us this in school. If they did it was something that was so simple that they did not spend a lot of time on. It is the most important thing about money and other assets. It is so simple why so many people and so few are buying assets. The word of God said my people are destroyed by a lack of knowledge. We are taught to be consumers to spend every penny we get our hands on and buy liability to look like you have money. However, a lot of us can't afford the things we have and get credit cards to help us get further into debt. So we look good but what you see is all we have.

No money in the bank, no investments and we are about one month away from being homeless. If your income stopped for a month everything would be taken away from you and you would be homeless. This is the state of most inner city people. Only one month away from poor. The problem is a lack of assets in our lives of any kind.

People Assets

There are all kinds of assets but I believe the best ones are the people assets that add to your life like a mentor. Many in the inner city do not have mentors beside mom and sometimes dad if he's around. A mentor is someone in your life who knows more than you and has sound wisdom. Age is not a judge of a mentor always because you have a lot of old fools. It has to do with where the person is getting their information from and is it working for them in the present. Did it work for others in the past and can it work for me in the future. In other words, it's timeless wisdom. The one that has it can be a good mentor. There are many people in your life that can be assets. You have to hear their words and watch their actions. I said people assets are the most important because of the relationships you can have and time you can spend with them. That is so valuable. People assets sometime make you uncomfortable when you're around them because of the wisdom they have.

You need to look for these people and talk to them. Ask for advice in all areas of your life. Sometimes they can be teachers. True teachers love to see people learn. Most teachers in the school system within the inner city are there for the money and the benefits and job security. A True teacher will light up when they see you learn. They love it and it gives them great joy to know that they are helping their kids. Businessmen, and women who have made it in their business share insight.

The one thing about mentors is they have a lot of words inside of them so you have to be careful of what you ask them. Get a list of thought out questions together that you would like to know about and ask smart questions. I use to have a boss who was older than me and he had so much wisdom and knowledge of the food industry. He could talk for hours about the good old days and I would be held captive until he finished talking.

However, I got smart and said I will control what we talk about. So I would always start the conversation with something I wanted to learn or know about. I would get a pen and paper and let him talk and I would write down the important points he would make. It was a great way to get information I had little or no knowledge about. If I had a question he didn't have the answer for, he would do some research and get back to me with the answer to my question. You must learn to use whatever resources are around you to your advantage.

Liability People

These people are all around you. The doggers, the complainers, the dream killers, the unbelievers, the critics, the pessimist, the jealous, in the hood we call them haters. These people take things out of your life and do not add anything back.   This type of person is a liability and you should avoid spending long periods of time with them. They will bring you down, kill your dreams and lower your self-esteem. I refer to them as toxic people. Always have something bad to say about everything and always talking about someone in a bad way. Stay away from toxic people even if its family as much as you possibly can. They are liabilities in your life. So it is not hard. Assets add to your life and liabilities take away from your life. We must apply this principle to everything in life. Buy assets and get away from liabilities and you will be successful. It will take time to change the way you think, but it will happen.

You have been brain washed for so long to think the wrong way about money and people. We must start slow and be steady to get back on track. A good idea would be to start with a friend you trust. You and this friend should compare each other's assets and liabilities. Concentrate and focus on the things that will bring you both more assets. Look at your money, what assets do you really have? Something that puts money into your pocket, not take it out. If your job is the only asset you have, you have got a lot of work to do. Don't be discouraged; start with saving a little money every time you get paid. Learn how to stop spending every penny each time you get paid. Once you're comfortable with saving and you have saved a sizable amount like $1,000 or more, start researching investment that might interest you.

You don't need a lot of money to invest in stocks or bonds. Also look into 401k plans at your job and any other investment plans your job may offer at very little cost to you. Start to pay your bills consistently. Rule number one is to pay you first. Most people don't realize the government takes up to 50% of what you earn in taxes. Yes, I said up to 50%. The reality is, you work four to six months for the government and six to eight months for yourself. This is a hard statement to digest but it is true. So you must pay yourself first. Here is a system of paying bills off totally:

1. Gather all of your bills
2. Pay the minimum payment on all them except one
3. For the one send double, or triple the amount due until it is completely paid
4. Take the money that you would have paid that bill with and add it to another one of your bills until it's completely paid.
5. Continue until all the bills are paid in full

This bill paying system works and you can be debt free in half the time if you would have paid your bills the regular way. Once you become free of debt, increase your savings and investments. You may want to buy a home for investment property. You can rent it out and/or live in it or both. You can also start a small business in your home. This will help with the entire tax burden. The key is you must do something to get you out of the "rat race".

The month-to-month bills and working for paycheck to pay check is not a good kind of life. [That kind of life is a trap that has 90% of people fall into and never gets paycheck starts with change the way we think about money.] We must begin to think out of the box, out of the American dream or a better term is American nightmare. We have been feed lies and it has taken on the roll of truth since the slavery system. Work hard and pay bill, when you retire you collect social security and live happily ever after.

Approximately 25% of us never make it to 65 years of age and narrow it down to just black men and the percentage increases. It's like chasing the wind, you never can get hold of it. The solution is thinking differently about your money and the people you love.

Remember this rule: people first, then money. Think of the people you love and care for each day and what would happen if you were not able to provide. Yes, begin with end in mind always. This is a standard of living that looks at the end first. If you continue to do what you've been doing what will be the end result of your actions?

Divide each area into categories:

1. Home life
2. Relationships
3. Work
4. Finances
5. Health

Examining each area, see what changes need to be made and make them? Examine your money, can you see yourself debt free? Wouldn't you like living on positive income at your age now and not when you reach 70 plus years? You don't want to be barely making it, month to month.

It is our choice, your actions, and your will to determine where you are financially in 20 to 30 years from now. Start today changing things doing things differently in your life. Get a plan and start today it will change your life.

True Success

What is success in your life? Many people have different ideas about success. You however, have to define what success is to you. Once you discover what success is, write it down and make it detailed and start today. You should start with the most important things like relationships. I believe this is the most important key to success. Your relationship with God is first. Then you have your family, friends, associates, and co-workers. When you spend time with them make it quality. Treat that time as if it might be the last day you will ever see them. Remember, tomorrow is not promised to any of us, but you have today. Make it the very best like it may be the last one. Your relationships will deepen and you will find much joy in everyday things you take for granted. Life is very short. The time we have here must be used wisely.

Many people think money is what makes them successful but that idea is so far from the truth. We must view money as a tool. When we use money to help others, the tool is being used in a correct way. Of course you can buy things with money like homes, cars, toys, however, the happiness these things bring only last for a very short time. Then something bigger and better comes along and you want that new thing. When you help someone who may be in great need, that action can change someone's life and this act will add to your life forever. Here is my definition of success:

To touch everyone's life I come in contact with in a positive way; to live each day like it was the last and never take for granted the wonderful people God has put in my life; to have all my needs met and to have enough to meet the needs of numerous others. I also want to raise productive children who will impact their world by what I have taught them. I want to find total inner peace in my God, my body. I want to be healthy and to live life fulfilling my God-given purpose.

Your definition of success may be different. Most people don't know what success is and unfortunately they will never find out. People are chasing the wrong things in life like chasing the wind. You must define the things, which are most important. Here is a way to begin to find answers. Imagine if your doctor said you only have a year to live. The things you would do in that year would be the most important things. Do them now and all the time and you will have a successful life.

Affirmation

_____

_____

_____

_____

_____

Success Goal

_____

_____

_____

_____

_____

The Mind Chapter #18

You are not your thoughts!! You are not your thoughts!! You are not your thoughts!!! Here is an exercise to try. Go into a dark room with no music or any other sounds and close your eyes; just start to listen to your thoughts as if someone was speaking to you. Your mind will start to race and so many thoughts will come to your mind that it will seem crazy. The brain is a tool that we can use to help us make decision, but it is a tool that must be used. Believe it or not most people allow their brains to use them. They are control by their thoughts and that is not how it supposed to be.

Have you ever had a thought come to your mind that made you laugh or feel sad or mad? They are only thoughts! The true you is the listener. The listener can hear the thought and decide to except or reject it. It is as simply as that, it is your choice. Once you learn that you have the ability to control your thoughts it will completely change your life. The Word of God says we can take every thought captive and make it obey Christ in us. When our minds are controlled we are really unconscious and are moving by impulse. This is insane. 90% or more of the people in this world are walking around insane, being led by the tool (brain) that is supposed to help you not rule you. This is why so many people are doing whatever comes to the mind like being gay.

No one in their right mind can say it is natural for a man and a man to come together and have sex. The parts don't fit. However, in the mind the thoughts say it looks like fun or let me try it out. A lot of people do because we have a rebellious nature. We justify it by saying we are born like this. It is a lie when are thoughts are in control. There are people who think it is right to kill for pleasure. They see a girl, think she's pretty and the mind says I will take her. Do you think that is right? NO! The mind has all kinds of crazy thoughts that come to it if you are being led by the mind. Being mind led you are capable of doing anything that comes to your mind. You must take the thoughts and judge them by the of the thought, and your spirit and take them captive and make them obey. People who are mind led are dangerous!!!! To themselves and others. Beware!!

How to stop being Mind lead

I will tell you a great secret. Meditation is Key! The Bible says that we should think on the thing that are good, righteous, and peaceful and of good report. What you fill your mind with is what will control your thoughts. It is of utmost importance that you learn to meditate. A good way to start is with slowing down your thoughts. This is difficulty but it can be done with practice. Try practice being alone. Some people have a hard time with themselves being alone. The reasons could be low self-esteem, self hate, and maybe you look like someone in your family you hate. It could be many reasons like abuse, un-forgiveness of someone. When you don't forgive you retain the sin of the unforgiving person and become like them. There are many, many reasons why someone can't stand to be alone. Here is the key: you must first force yourself to confront this thing that is holding you captive. YOURSELF. Start to make yourself spend time alone; at least one hour a day when you can be undisturbed. Take a pen with you and write what comes to mind. Don't think about it just begin to write until the thoughts stop coming as fast. This is how you slow down your mind. Look at the paper you wrote on and you will see how out of control your thoughts are and why you must get them under control immediately.

Do the exercises until you start to enjoy this time alone. Once your thoughts began to slow down then you will be able to meditate. Meditation is controlled thinking. You will start to feed your mind thoughts and think about them over and over. Start with simple things like breathing. Just listen to your in and out breathing. When you breathe in – a good thought and when you breathe out – a bad thought. Breathe in peace, breath out confusion. Breathe in faith, breath out doubt. Continue doing this until you feel the peace and faith in your body. You will know when this happens. It will be when your thoughts come under control and you can choose the thought you want to keep and the thought you don't want. Why do this you ask? It will help you in every area of your life. God has given us the ability to make decisions and it is the most powerful gift you have. When you use it to direct your mind, wonderful, powerful things happen. A peace that surpasses all understanding comes over you. In that peace is God's presence and his voice. He wants to direct you. Be still and know Him intimately...

Chapter #19 the making of a slave (8 point from the Willie lynch letter)

THE PLAN: a foolproof method that is put into place. That will keep your slaves mentally enslaved for at least 300 years (that is 4.2 generation) First divide and conquer turn the light skin slaves against the dark skin slaves. The old slaves against the young, and the house slave against the field slave. Teach them to only love and respect and need the master. If you use this method for one year they will perpetually distrust each other for life. Put the female in the head of house position make her control the family. Have her teach her male child to obey and to be week minded for her own safety. Then Tar and feather the biggest and strongest male slave put him between two horses set him on fire and Rips him in two pieces in front of all to impart great fear...

Brake any rebellion of the male slave with a whip and hunger like a horse. Do this in front of all to see, put the fear of god in them. Remove the male influence form the family the male slave must be raised to be mentally dependent on the master

Control the language and talk of place of origin (Africa). Take away the influences traditions, religions and customs. Teach them the English language only speck it. Don't ever teach them to read or write. Make it a crime to read books. They portray it, punishable by death and castration. This will take the ability to communicate with each other without us understanding.

Take their names form them, and give them your names this make them your property. Brand them with hot irons like animals, and take away their clothing no native garments. Teach them the word of Jesus and tell them to obey all of the word of god. But we the master does not have to flow the same religion. Because if we flow the words we teach them we cannot keep them as slave they will then be our brothers. Keep the body working but control the mind brake the will to resist or to ask questions. Breed Workers not thinkers this system is still in place and will last for 300 years they will mentally enslave them self for 4.2 Generation

This is the reason the jails are full and the paints or sagging and the heads are so empty now that you know do not blame the white man. We must change the way we think. The one that came up with the systems are long dead. We are doing this to ourselves. Mental slaves...

Chapter # 20 Escaping Mental Slavery (It's your choice)

From the last chapter you can see what we are up against a system set up to keep all of us enslaved black & white alike but the good news is that it can be broken here is a 12 step program

The first step in any plain is to first admit that there is a problem. We all wear bread to ignore the hard things in life and to ask ourselves the hard questions. Just admit I am a mental slave… And I want to be free.

Start to retrain our minds READ anything that you can get your hands on that uplifts, motivates and inspirer you to think for yourself. Trust GOD NOT MAN the word of god that was taught to us is not a bad thing there are principles and law that can be very helpful in our transformation.

Stop killing each other, learn that the hate and division that was pasted down from the system is not the way it should be. Divide and conquer is a thing of the pass.   UNITE AND PROSPER IS THE THEME OF THE FUTURE.

Support minority business buy in your community if the products are not there open a business and hirer your neighbors. The reason they intergraded us in the pass is not because they wanted to help. They saw that we had our own school and business and banks. We were becoming self-depended and financially independent. This would have broken the system …

Fathers get on your jobs. Get involved in your kids life teach them what it is to be men of God. I am a part of a mentoring program we need more men. Calling all men and woman. We need mentors in the life of our sons and daughters. If you are not a part of the solution you're the problem. We can't sit in the barbershops and beauty salon and talk about the problems in our communities we must take an active role in changing things. We can't wait for Obama to save us. We must save our children and ourselves. Go to the schools and demand change if they are substandard. Say this with me is it is going to be it is up to me …

We need to start asking our self-hard questions. Like what is my purpose, who am I, what is the cause and effect of my actions, what does my future look like if I continue to stay mentally enslaved. We must seek God until we find out the answer to this question.

Protect your time Start to spend time with asset people these people add to your life. When you are around them they make you feel hopeful and live. They will some time make you feel uncomfortable if you are not doing anything to change your live but this is necessary to change your mind set. Don't spend a lot of time with Liability people that are always taking form you, and complaining about their life but refuse to do anything about it. This is a drain on your mental transformation and a waste of the valuable time that God has given you we must spend our time wisely. It is not a renewable asset when its gone it gone you can't get spent time back you must learn to invest it not spend it …

Work for seed not for greed we must learn not to work for Money. But for knowledge and SEED yes that is right seed we must learn to be givers .use the principles in the word of God to help free you. The money we go to work for is never enough. So we must take a lesson form the farmers if he has an ear of corn is that enough to feed his family no; but if he take the same ear of corn. And take the corneal and plant them in good ground he can feed the whole block. This is seedtime and harvest Principle. You give a little and gain 10, 50, or 100 times what you have given. The word works try it.

Learn to be led by the Holy Spirit not by the mind. Your spirit can take every thought captive and make it obey Christ that lives in you. But you have to feed your spirit to make it stronger. The Sprit eats the word of God and prayer and fasting also meditation on the word. You must feed him daily some time a couple times a day and see how you will grow this is the renewing of the mind and whom the Son set free is free indeed.

Know the real Enemy: DON'T THINK THIS IS A BLACK OR WHITE THING Our real enemy has been enslaving man and woman for a long time and he uses all kinds of trick to divide and conquer. But the word says we fight not against human beings but against the wicked spiritual forces in the heavenly world, the rulers, authorities and cosmic powers of this dark age and there is no way you can win outside of Christ the odds are stacked to high against you. This is why he give us armor so read Ephesians 6:13 to 6:18 this tell you about your spiritual weapon's

We must realize that nothing is Impossible that we can do all things thru God who give us Power. We may be in a really bad state because of year of our mind being enslaved. Our life can be out of control. And the damage to our family can be devastating. But with faith the size of a mustard seed and with God help we can move Mountains. There will be weapons formed against us but they will not prosper.

Use the mind stop letting it use us. Slavery came from a mind of a man influents' by the evil one. So it can be broken by a man's mind that is influents by the Great I AM, he is all you need and more. Your peace that surpasses all understanding, the all sufficient ONE, BECAUSE YOU ARE MORE THEN A CONQUER IN CHRIST WHO GIVE YOU STRENGTH this means you have already win the battle you just have to get that truth into your Mind all the hard work was done for you at Calvary. We are already Free the chains have already been removed. You are released so start to walk in that Freedom it is up to you What a man Think so shell he Become so let's say it together I am Free, I AM FREE

A note to the reader

It been over Twenty years of walking with God it is not easy. Those who live in Christ will suffer persecution, hardship, troubles, Trials, Setbacks & disappointments. There is one thing I do know that even when I walked away from him. He never left me.my life started out a mess I was lost. But God find me pick me up dusted me off and gave me a new life. Form the projects to dropping out of school God have allowed me to attend the two best culinary Schools in the USA. He has allowed me to open my own restaurant and catering business.

Making over 120,000 a year this may not be a lot to some but from where I started it had to be God. Herbie Fields that my teachers said, "I was never going to be nothing." "I know the plans I have for you sayeth the Lord.'" Jeremiah 29:11 (Paraphrased). God has the final say.

In my career I had the opportunity to cater parties for the ex president of the United States Bill Clinton, also Spike Lee, Eddie murphy, Gladys Night & many more. The guy who was so afraid to read I front of the class. I have had the opportunity to teach at Fairleigh Dickinson University. I also opened up my own school for cooking. I reserved numerous awards and citation for my work. Form Mayor, Senators, and newspapers I said these things not to boost on me but my boost is in the lord that never gave up on me in the mental salve state he set me free. And I know he is still working on me. There is no limit to what God can do. I can't believe I am writing a book. I leave you with this trust in the Lord with all your heart and lean not to your understanding, but in all your way trust him and he will direct your path.

Thank you for taking time out to read my book.

Affirmation

_____

_____

_____

_____

_____

Writing affirmations, help us to be accountable, and equipped. Make sure you take time to write yours, and read them whenever you feel you're falling off track, and your mind needs to be renewed.

Herbert. L. Fields